# FAST MAMA

## *SlowCooker*

### 70 FAVORITES FOR YOUR FAST-PACED FAMILY

# FAST MAMA
## *SlowCooker*

### 70 FAVORITES FOR YOUR FAST-PACED FAMILY

BRENDA STANLEY · SUZIE ROBERTS

CHRISTI SILBAUGH · MICHELE VILSECK

KRISTENA EDEN · ANNALISE THOMAS

CARLENE DUDA · LYUBA BROOKE

FRONT TABLE BOOKS · AN IMPRINT OF CEDAR FORT, INC. | SPRINGVILLE, UTAH

ISBN 13: 978-1-4621-1988-2

Published by Front Table Books, an imprint of Cedar Fort, Inc.
2373 W. 700 S., Springville, UT 84663
Distributed by Cedar Fort, Inc., www.cedarfort.com

LIBRARY OF CONGRESS CATALOGING-IN-PUBLICATION DATA

Names: Stanley, Brenda- author. | Roberts, Suzie- author. | Eden, Kristena- author.
Title: Fast Mama, Slow Cooker / Brenda Stanley, Suzie Roberts, and Kristena Eden
Description: Springville, Utah : Front Table Books, an imprint of Cedar Fort, Inc., [2017]
Identifiers: LCCN 2016055145 | ISBN 9781462119882 (layflat : acid-free paper)
Subjects: LCSH: Cooking (Slow) | LCGFT: Cookbooks.
Classification: TX827 .S72 2017 | DDC 641.5/884
LC record available at https://lccn.loc.gov/2016055145

Cover and page design by Priscilla Chaves
Cover design © 2017 Cedar Fort, Inc.
Edited by Deborah Spencer

Printed in the United States of America

10 9 8 7 6 5 4 3 2 1

Printed on acid-free paper

# Contents

# Introduction

Mothers know that it's always nice to find some time to unwind together as a family at the dinner table. Too often, though, family meals turn into a whirlwind itself, and instead of a few minutes of peace, these moments can be just as hectic as the rest of the day.

But no more! Using your slow cooker will change everything.

Turn your mealtime into something that everyone looks forward to! The recipes in this book will help you save time, make delicious food, and help everyone to focus on the most important thing: time spent together as a family. From breakfast dishes to delectable desserts, this book has everything you need to prepare fast, healthy, comfort food.  Needing only minimal prep and a few hours for the ingredients to cook, your slow cooker can be your best friend in the kitchen—always helpful and always bringing something tasty to your table.

The authors of this book hope that you enjoy this book as much as they did in creating the recipes.

Bon appetite!

# A Quick History of Slow Cooking

**The original version** of the slow cooker began with the use of iron pots hung over a fire or buried in hot coals. The food was simmered for many hours. This was a great way to tenderize tough meats and dense, fibrous vegetables. It was also considered cost efficient.

**The Naxon Utilities Company of Chicago** was the first to manufacture a version of what we use today. It was originally called the Naxon Beanery. It was composed of a ceramic pot that was fitted in a metal pan surrounded by heating elements.

**The Rival Company** bought out Naxon in 1970. Just a year later, Rival took the concept of the Beanery and produced an appliance with a similar function called the Crock-Pot. In 1974, Rival also created the removable ceramic pot, which became useful in both storing and cleanup. The Rival and Crock-Pot brands are now owned by Sunbeam Products, yet many other companies produce their own slow cookers.

# Timely Tips

Unless otherwise specified, always cover the slow cooker with a tight-fitting lid while cooking.

Don't open the lid of the cooker to check on things. It takes 15 minutes to reach the desired level of heat again.

The slow cooker should be between half and two-thirds full. Too much or too little food will affect the outcome of the dish. For meals that serve between four and ten people, use a 5- to 6-quart slow cooker, which is considered standard size.

Thaw meats before placing in the slow cooker.

Avoid placing the hot cooker insert directly onto a cold surface or in cold water. The shock could make it crack.

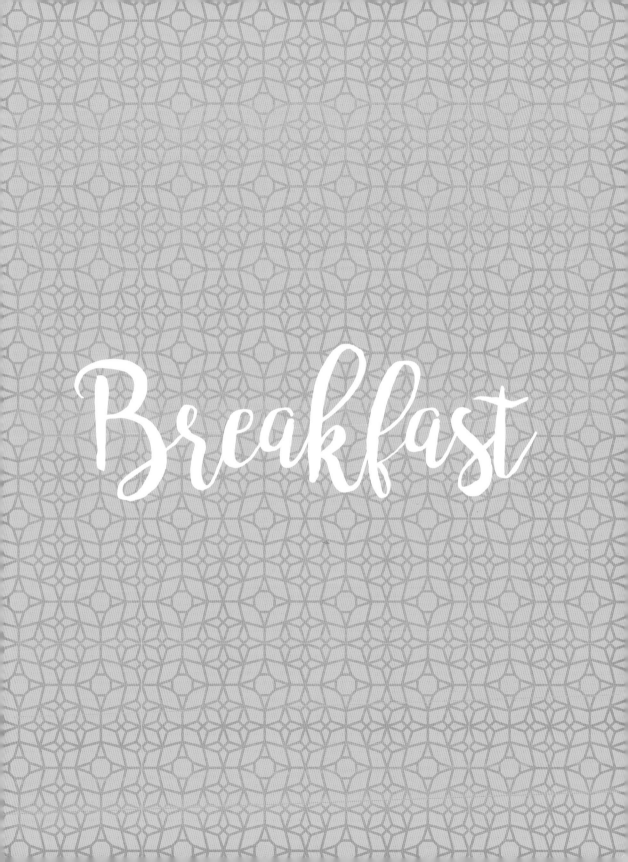

# Breakfast

# Pumpkin Pie Slow Cooker Oatmeal

## 5–6 SERVINGS

4 cups water

½ cup milk
(or almond milk)

2 cups old-fashioned rolled oats

1 cup pumpkin purée

½–1 cup firmly packed brown sugar (to taste)

2 Tbsp. butter or coconut oil

1 Tbsp. pumpkin pie spice

1 Tbsp. cinnamon

½ tsp. salt

If you've never experienced slow cooker oatmeal, you are in for a treat. I can't even tell you how amazing it is to wake up to the smell of this oatmeal. Add in a programmable coffee maker, and you've got hands-free morning bliss right there!

Throw this easy breakfast together in 2 minutes before you go to bed, turn the slow cooker on LOW and go to sleep. You will wake up to a delicious, hearty breakfast the whole family will love!

But be warned . . . you may just find yourself wanting to top this breakfast with a mound of fresh whipped cream and some toasted pecans!

◊ Stir all of the ingredients together in the slow cooker. Cook on low* overnight, at least 8 hours. (*If you think your slow cooker runs hot, cook this on keep warm overnight to keep it from burning!)

◊ When it is done, give it a good stir so everything comes together and serve with your favorite oatmeal toppings!

You can store any leftover oatmeal in individual containers in the fridge to reheat for super quick breakfasts later in the week, or scoop into greased muffin tins, freeze, and then pop out into a freezer bag for even longer storage!

# Overnight Oatmeal

**8 SERVINGS**

2 cups old-fashioned or steel-cut oats

4 cups milk

1 cup water

½ tsp. salt

raisins (optional)

So creamy and wholesome, this dish is the perfect start to the day!

◊ Place all the ingredients into the slow cooker and mix well. Cook on low about 6 hours.

# Creamy Slow Cooker Oatmeal

**6 SERVINGS**

4 ½ cups water

1 ½ cups oats

1 ½ cups half-and-half

1 tsp. vanilla

a pinch of salt

½ cup brown sugar

This old-time favorite will save you some time in the morning! Start this oatmeal the evening before and it will be ready when your are.

◊ Just before going to bed, combine water and oats in slow cooker. Set to low, cover, and let cook overnight. In the morning, stir in half-and-half, vanilla, and salt. Scoop into bowls. Sprinkle each with brown sugar.

# Florentine Breakfast Casserole

**8–10 SERVINGS**

1½ cups shredded cheddar cheese

1 (9-oz.) package fresh spinach, chopped

1 cup cubed white bread

1 cup sliced fresh mushrooms

½ cup sliced green onions

6 eggs

1½ cups milk

½ cup heavy cream

1 tsp. salt

1 tsp. black pepper

1 tsp. garlic powder

I love the combination of fresh spinach and mushrooms.

◊ Lightly grease the slow cooker. Layer ½ of the cheddar cheese and the spinach, bread, mushrooms, and green onions in bottom of the slow cooker. Whisk together the eggs, milk, cream, salt, pepper, and garlic powder. Pour egg mixture over top of everything in slow cooker. Sprinkle the remaining cheese on top. Cook on high about 2 hours.

# Four-Ingredient Breakfast Casserole

**6–8 SERVINGS**

1 lb. mild bulk sausage

1 (32-oz.) bag frozen hash browns

2 cups shredded cheddar cheese

10 eggs

This dish may only have four ingredients, but the taste is savory and delicious.

◊ Brown and crumble the sausage. Drain. Place ⅓ of the hash browns in the bottom of the slow cooker followed by ⅓ of the cheese and topped with ⅓ of the sausage. Repeat the layers. Pour the eggs over top. Cook on low 8–10 hours.

# Train Wreck for Breakfast

**12 SERVINGS**

1 lb. ground sausage

6 eggs

1 (12-oz.) pkg. hash browns

1 (8-oz.) pkg. favorite grated cheese

Super simple, nutritious, and pleases everyone. Good in a crock pot and in a dutch oven.

◊ Thoroughly mix all ingredients except cheese in slow cooker, and cook on high for 3 hours. Top with grated cheese and cook for 20 minutes more.

Entrée:
Beef

# Sweet & Sour Meatballs

## MEATBALLS

1 lb. ground beef

½ cup dry bread crumbs

¼ cup milk

¾ tsp. salt

½ tsp. Worcestershire sauce

¼ tsp. pepper

¼ cup onion, minced

1 egg

## SAUCE

½ cup brown sugar

2 tsp. dry mustard

½ tsp. nutmeg

1 cup ketchup

This is a welcome change from your typical sweet and sour recipes.

◊ Mix all meatball ingredients together and form balls. Bake on a cookie sheet at 400° for 20 minutes. Mix sauce ingredients together. If freezing, see directions below. Otherwise, place meatballs in a slow cooker and pour sauce over them. Mix to coat meatballs and cook on low for 2–3 hours.

**FREEZING DIRECTIONS:**

*Place meatballs in a freezer bag and pour sauce over them.*

## SHOPPING LIST FOR 10 MEALS

10 lbs. ground beef

5 cups dry bread crumbs

2½ cups milk

2½ Tbsp. salt

5 tsp. Worcestershire sauce

2½ tsp. pepper

3 large onions

10 eggs

5 cups brown sugar

abt. ¼ cup dry mustard

5 tsp. nutmeg

abt. 4 (24-oz.) bottles ketchup (total of 80 oz.)

# Italian Meatball Subs

## MEATBALLS

1 lb. lean ground beef

1 cup Italian bread crumbs

½ cup shredded Parmesan cheese

1 Tbsp. fresh minced parsley (or 1 tsp. dried)

1 garlic clove, minced

½ cup milk

1 egg

## SAUCE

2 (15-oz.) cans tomato sauce

1 (29-oz.) can crushed Italian tomatoes

½ cup shredded Parmesan cheese

2 envelopes spaghetti sauce seasoning

## TO SERVE

hogi buns

shredded mozzarella or provolone cheese

The spaghetti sauce seasoning thickens the sauce perfectly and adds the right balance of flavor.

◊ Combine meatball ingredients in a large bowl. Set aside. In another large bowl, combine the sauce ingredients and stir until well mixed. Pour about ⅓ of the sauce mixture in the bottom of a large slow cooker. Form the meatballs from the meat mixture and put them in a single layer in the sauce in the slow cooker. Add some sauce to cover the tops and sides of the meatballs. Add more meatballs and cover with more sauce. When all the meatballs are in the slow cooker, pour the rest of the sauce on and cover. Cook on low for 8 hours or high for 4 hours.

### FREEZING DIRECTIONS:

*After cooking, allow to cool. Pour into freezer bags. To serve, heat in a large saucepan. Serve on buns with shredded cheese on top. Include a bag of 1½ cups of shredded cheese and a package of buns.*

# Stuffed Italian Flank Steak

**6 SERVINGS**

2 eggs, beaten

½ cup Italian bread crumbs

1 (2-lb.) flank steak, pounded to ¼ inch

1 tsp. salt

½ tsp. pepper

5 slices bacon

1 cup Italian cheese blend, shredded

2 Tbsp. oil

2 (26-oz.) jars marinara sauce

Flank steak is full of flavor, and, combined with a smoky and savory stuffing, your family will love this meal!

◊ Mix together the eggs and the bread crumbs in a small bowl. Sprinkle both sides of the meat with salt and pepper. Pat the bread crumb mixture over one side of the flank steak, leaving about a 1-inch border around edges. Top bread crumbs with the bacon slices. Sprinkle with shredded cheese. Starting from one long side, tightly roll flank steak using string or toothpicks to secure.

◊ Heat oil in skillet and sear the stuffed flank steak in the hot oil until well browned on all sides. Transfer the meat to the slow cooker and pour marinara sauce over meat to cover. Cook on low 6–8 hours. Slice and serve with marinara.

# Smothered Steak

1½ lbs. stew meat (steak)

⅓ cup flour

½ tsp. salt

¼ tsp. pepper

1 small chopped, onion

3 (8-oz.) cans tomato sauce

3 Tbsp. soy sauce

1 can french-style green beans

## SHOPPING LIST FOR 10 MEALS

15 lbs. stew meat (steak)

3⅓ cups flour

5 tsp. salt

2½ tsp. pepper

10 small onions

30 (8-oz.) cans tomato sauce or 15 (16-oz.) cans

about 2 cups soy sauce

10 cans french-style green beans

10 small bags rice

This saucy dish is a real treat after a long day's work.

◊ Put steak, flour, salt, and pepper in a slow cooker. Stir well to coat meat. Add all remaining ingredients. Cover and cook 6–8 hours. Serve over rice, if desired.

### FREEZING DIRECTIONS:

*Place flour, salt, and pepper in a freezer bag. Place meat in the bag and shake to coat. Mix all remaining ingredients except green beans together and pour over meat. Freeze flat in freezer. Include the can of green beans with the meal. Mix the beans in the slow cooker with the other ingredients to cook. You may want to include a bag of rice with this meal also.*

# Creamy Mushroom Steak

**6 SERVINGS**

⅓ cup flour

½ tsp. salt

½ tsp. pepper

6 cube steaks

2 Tbsp. oil

2 (10.5-oz.) cans cream of mushroom soup

½ cup milk

So tasty you'll want to serve this with rice or noodles to soak up the gravy.

◊ Mix together the flour, salt, and pepper. Coat the steaks in the flour and shake off excess. Brown the steaks on both sides in hot oil. Place in the slow cooker. Mix together the soup and milk and pour over top. Cook on low for 6 hours.

**FREEZING DIRECTIONS:**

Place flour, salt, and pepper in a freezer bag. Place meat in the bag and shake to coat. Mix all remaining ingredients except green beans together and pour over meat. Freeze flat in freezer. Include the can of green beans with the meal. Mix the beans in the slow cooker with the other ingredients to cook. You may want to include a bag of rice with this meal also.

# Spicy Asian Short Ribs

**4 SERVINGS**

3–4 lbs. beef short ribs

½ cup soy sauce

⅓ cup brown sugar

¼ cup rice vinegar

1 tsp. garlic, minced

1 tsp. ground ginger

1 tsp. sesame oil

½ tsp. crushed red pepper flakes

1 cup carrots cut into 1-inch chunks

½ head of cabbage, cut into quarters

2 Tbsp. cornstarch

¼ cup coarsely chopped green onions

This sweet and spicy dish is perfect with rice. The meat is succulent and tender.

◊ Trim excess fat from ribs and place in the slow cooker. Mix together the soy sauce, sugar, vinegar, garlic, ginger, sesame oil, and red pepper.

◊ Place ribs in slow cooker and pour mixture over ribs. Place carrots and cabbage on top. Cook on low 7–8 hours. Transfer the cabbage, short ribs, and carrots to plate and cover with foil. Skim the fat from the cooking liquid and discard. Turn the slow cooker to high. In a small bowl, whisk together the cornstarch with ¼ cup of water until smooth. Whisk into the cooking liquid and cook until thickened. Spoon the sauce over the short ribs and vegetables and sprinkle with the green onions.

SUZIE ROBERTS | BUSY MOMS ON THE GO

# Best Sunday Roast

## 8–10 SERVINGS

1 rump roast

3 pkgs. beef gravy mix

1 pkg. dry Italian dressing mix

1 pkg. dry ranch dressing mix

3 cups water

This is my family's favorite Sunday dinner.

◊ If freezing, see sidebar. Otherwise, place roast in a slow cooker. In a small bowl, mix together the remaining ingredients. Pour over roast. Cook on low for 6–8 hours. The roast will fall apart, and the gravy is delicious to have over mashed potatoes!

**FREEZING DIRECTIONS:**

*Place roast in a gallon-sized freezer bag. Pour mixture over and freeze.*

**SHOPPING LIST FOR 10 MEALS**

10 rump roasts

30 pkgs. beef gravy mix

10 pkgs. dry Italian dressing mix

10 pkgs. dry ranch dressing mix

---

BRENDA STANLEY | THAT'S A LOT OF CROCK!

# Grandma's Pot Roast

## 6–8 SERVINGS

1 (3-lb.) chuck roast

1 tsp. garlic salt

1 tsp. pepper

3 cups beef broth

2 cups carrots, chopped

2 cups potatoes, chopped

1 cup celery, chopped

No frills, but always a favorite. This will melt in your mouth.

◊ Sprinkle the roast with garlic salt and pepper. Place in slow cooker and cover with broth. Cook on low for 6 hours. Place vegetables in pot and cook another 4 hours.

# Roasted Garlic Pumpkin Pot Roast

**8–10 SERVINGS**

1 head garlic

1 (3–4-lb.) boneless chuck roast

1 (2-lb.) pumpkin

2 large carrots

1 large yellow onion

5–6 cups of beef stock

5–6 stems of thyme

2 (4–5-inch) rosemary stems

2 bay leaves

1 Tbsp. Worcestershire sauce

salt

fresh cracked pepper

**PREP TIME: 40 MINUTES**

**COOK TIME: 8–10 HOURS**

Winter is the best time to break out your slow cooker and make some easy, comforting dishes to warm your tummy and your soul. This slow cooker pot roast is no doubt one of those dishes. It's infused with roasted garlic flavor and made with the best fall vegetable, the pumpkin. Flavor added by roasted garlic is well worth the extra time put in preparing it.

◊ First roast the garlic. Peel most of the skin off the head of garlic. Cut off top of the garlic, just enough to expose tips of all the cloves. Wrap garlic in aluminum foil and place on a baking sheet. Roast at 400 degrees for 35–40 minutes. Garlic should be soft and golden. Not to mention also smelling amazing!

◊ Place chuck roast in a slow cooker. Peel, seed, and chop pumpkin. Chop carrots and onion as well. Spread veggies around the meat.

◊ In a large pot, heat up beef stock and add thyme, rosemary, bay leaves, Worcestershire sauce, salt, pepper, and meat of the roasted garlic. Bring to a boil and taste to see if you need a little more salt or spice.

◊ Pour the mixture over the meat in the slow cooker. Cover and cook on low for 8–10 hours.

# Beef Bourguignon

**6–8 SERVINGS**

½ cup flour

1 tsp. salt

½ tsp. pepper

4 lbs. beef chuck, cubed

3 Tbsp. oil

1 cup onion, chopped

1 cup mushrooms, sliced

1 cup fresh parsley, chopped

5 tsp. minced garlic

4 bay leaves

2 cups red wine vinegar

1 cup beef broth

Julia Child made this dish famous. Hers took hours of work. Yours will cook for hours while you are at work.

◊ Mix the flour, salt, and pepper. Dredge beef in flour mixture. Brown the beef in hot oil on all sides. Place the beef in the slow cooker and add the remaining ingredients. Cook on low 4–6 hours.

---

# Beefy Country Casserole

**4 SERVINGS**

½ lb. ground beef

2 Tbsp. real bacon bits

½ onion, chopped

1 (8-oz.) can tomato sauce

½ cup water

½ tsp. chili powder

¼ tsp. salt

¼ tsp. pepper

⅔ cup long-grain rice, uncooked

1 (15.25-oz.) can corn, drained

½ cup green bell pepper, chopped

This dish combines traditional flavors into a delicious and hearty meal.

◊ Crumble the ground beef evenly over bottom of a 3½-quart slow cooker. Sprinkle with bacon bits and then onion. In a medium bowl, combine tomato sauce, water, chili powder, salt, and black pepper; pour half over beef and onion layers. Sprinkle rice evenly over top, then corn. Top with remaining tomato sauce mixture, then bell pepper. Cook on low 5 hours or until rice is tender.

# Shredded Beef French Dip Sandwiches

1 rump roast

2 envelopes au jus mix

1 pkg. rolls
(6–8 deli rolls or
12–18 hard rolls)

**SHOPPING LIST
FOR 10 MEALS**

10 rump roasts

20 envelopes
au jus mix

10 pkgs. Rolls

Serve this with chips and carrot sticks to make your meal finger-friendly.

◊ Place rump roast in slow cooker and cook on medium for 3–6 hours until it shreds easily. Halfway through cooking, take the roast out, cut off the fat, and drain juices. Place back in slow cooker. Prepare au jus according to package directions and pour over roast. Cook for the remaining amount of time until it shreds. If freezing, see directions below. Otherwise, serve on rolls and dip in au jus.

**FREEZING
DIRECTIONS:**

*Place meat and prepared au jus in a freezer bag. Include a bag of rolls with this meal. To prepare this meal in bulk, you can place approximately 5 roasts in a large roaster oven.*

# Carne Asada Tacos

**4–6 SERVINGS**

2 tsp. olive oil

2 Tbsp. ground cumin

2 Tbsp. chili powder

2 tsp. salt

2 tsp. freshly cracked black pepper

2 lb. boneless beef steak

3 tomatoes, diced

2 jalapeño peppers, seeded and chopped

1 yellow onion, chopped

4 cloves garlic, chopped

1 (10.5-oz.) can beef broth

1 pkg. corn tortillas

taco toppings (lettuce, tomatoes, salsa, and so on)

Gluten-free is the perfect excuse for meat lovers to eat their favorite dish—steak! Here's one way to enjoy it tender and packed with flavor. Substitute chicken or pork if desired. Top with pico de gallo and serve with black beans and spanish rice.

◊ Grease a slow cooker with olive oil. In small bowl, combine the cumin, chili powder, salt, and black pepper. Sprinkle the spice mixture over the beef so that it is evenly coated and place in the crock pot.

◊ Place all cleaned and prepared vegetables in the slow cooker with the garlic. Add broth and cook on low for 8 hours or high for 4 hours.

◊ Shred the meat with 2 forks and drizzle with some of the braising liquid to keep the meat moist. Cover until ready to serve. Warm tortillas in a tortilla warmer or on a lightly greased frying pan. Stuff tortillas with shredded steak, pico de gallo, and other toppings as desired.

**FRESH HERBS:**

*Using fresh herbs is nutritious and a great way to enhance the flavor of your foods. They are like any other vegetable; simply wash, chop, and add to the recipe as directed!*

# Slow Cooker Cabbage Rolls

## 6 SERVINGS

12 cabbage leaves, green or Napa

1 cup cooked rice

1 large egg, beaten

¼ cup milk

¼ cup minced sweet onion

1 lb. extra-lean ground beef

1¼ tsp. salt

1¼ tsp. ground black pepper

1 (8-oz.) can tomato sauce

1 Tbsp. brown sugar

1 Tbsp. lemon juice

1 tsp. Worcestershire sauce

Slow cooker recipes are great for the multitasker in us all. Let these delicious cabbage rolls cook while you enjoy the more exciting side of life. These cabbage rolls are delicious and require no tying or complicated wrapping. Serve over rice.

◊ Bring a large pot of water to a boil. Boil cabbage leaves 2 minutes; drain.

◊ In a large bowl, combine rice, egg, milk, onion, ground beef, salt, and pepper.

◊ Place about ¼ cup of meat mixture in center of each cabbage leaf and roll up, tucking in ends. Place rolls in a slow cooker.

◊ In a small bowl, mix together tomato sauce, brown sugar, lemon juice, and Worcestershire sauce. Pour over cabbage rolls.

◊ Cover your crock pot, and cook on Low 8 to 9 hours or high for 4 hours.

# Hawaiian Burgers

**4 SERVINGS**

2 boxes rice mix of choice

4 Tbsp. brown sugar

1 cup or a handful fresh green beans

4 hamburger patties

4 slices cheese

4 slices pineapple, canned or fresh

All the flavors of the islands.

◊ Mix rice and brown sugar with 1½ cups water. Pour into slow cooker.

◊ Add green beans and top with hamburger patties.

◊ Cook on high 5 hours. Top with cheese slices and sliced pineapple (one of each per burger). Cook for 1 hour more.

# Entrée: Chicken

# Cheesy Italian Chicken

2 cans cream of chicken soup

¾ cup milk

¾ cup Italian bread crumbs

2 cups Monterey Jack cheese

4–6 boneless, skinless chicken breasts, cut in pieces

### SHOPPING LIST FOR 10 MEALS

20–30 lbs. boneless, skinless chicken breasts

20 cans cream of chicken soup

abt. 2 quarts milk

7½ cups Italian bread crumbs

5 lbs. shredded Monterey Jack cheese

10 small bags rice

Easy and cheesy—this is a dish that gets repeat requests!

◊ Mix soup, milk, bread crumbs, and cheese together. Add chicken pieces. Cook in slow cooker on low for 6–8 hours. Stir often so cheese doesn't stick to the bottom. Serve over rice or noodles.

### FREEZING DIRECTIONS:

Place chicken pieces in a freezer bag. Mix all other ingredients together and pour over chicken in the bag. You may want to include a bag of rice with this meal.

# Chicken Marengo

1 can tomato soup

1 can Golden Mushroom soup

1 can mushrooms, drained

½ cup chopped onion

6 boneless, skinless chicken breasts

### SHOPPING LIST FOR 10 MEALS

60 boneless, skinless chicken breasts (abt. 30 lbs.)

10 cans tomato soup

10 cans Golden Mushroom soup

10 cans mushrooms

5 onions

10 bags egg noodles

The combination of these ingredients makes a great flavorful chicken.

◊ Mix soups, mushrooms and onion. Pour mixture over chicken in slow cooker and cook on low for 6–8 hours. Serve over warm noodles.

**FREEZING DIRECTIONS:**

*Place chicken in freezer bag. Pour mixture over chicken and seal. Include a package of noodles with this meal.*

# Creamy Bacon Chicken

5–6 boneless, skinless chicken breasts

1 (3-oz.) pkg. precooked bacon bits (not artificial)

1 can roasted garlic cream of mushroom soup

1 can cream of mushroom soup

1 cup sour cream

½ cup flour

### SHOPPING LIST FOR 10 MEALS

abt. 30 lbs. boneless, skinless chicken breasts

10 (3-oz.) pkgs. precooked bacon bits (not artificial)

10 cans roasted garlic cream of mushroom soup

10 cans cream of mushroom soup

5 pints sour cream

5 cups flour

10 pkgs. egg noodles

Rich and creamy!

◊ Place chicken in slow cooker. Mix all remaining ingredients together and pour over chicken. Cook on low for 6–8 hours. Serve over egg noodles.

### FREEZING DIRECTIONS:

*Place chicken in a gallon-size freezer bag. Pour sauce mixture over chicken. Seal and freeze. You may want to include a bag of egg noodles with this meal.*

# Belle's Asian Chicken and Quinoa Lettuce Wraps

4 chicken thighs

½ cup Teriyaki Glaze (I like Kikkoman Teriyaki Baste and Glaze)

1½ cups water

½ cup quinoa

½ tsp. sesame oil

Pinch of crushed dried red pepper flakes

1 (8 ounce) can sliced water chestnuts, chopped

¼ cup chopped green onions

8 large romaine lettuce leaves, washed and patted dry

My Asian Chicken and Quinoa Lettuce Wraps is a satisfying and flavorful dish that is also high in protein and low in fat and calories . . . what could be better?

◊ Place the chicken and Teriyaki sauce in a slow cooker. Stir to coat the chicken. Cover and cook on low for 6 hours. Shred the chicken with 2 forks while still in the pot and mix well with the sauce. Add the chestnuts and mix well. Turn the slow cooker to warm. In a saucepan, bring water to a boil. Reduce heat. Stir in quinoa, sesame oil, and red pepper flakes, cover and simmer for about 15–20 minutes. Add quinoa to chicken mixture and stir well. Place a heaping spoonful on lettuce leaf and fold like a taco to eat.

# Divine Crockpot Chicken

5–6 boneless, skinless chicken breasts

1 can cream of celery soup

1 can cream of mushroom soup

1 envelope dry onion soup mix

1 tsp. dried parsley

### SHOPPING LIST FOR 10 MEALS

abt. 30 lbs. boneless, skinless chicken breasts

10 cans cream of celery soup

10 cans cream of mushroom soup

5 pkgs. (2 envelopes each) dry onion soup mix

3⅓ Tbsp. dried parsley

10 small bags of rice or egg noodles

Slow cooker meals are perfect for warm summer days because you don't have to heat up your oven.

◊ Place chicken in slow cooker. Mix all other ingredients together and pour over chicken. Cook on low for 4–6 hours. Serve over pasta or rice.

### FREEZING DIRECTIONS:

*Place chicken in a gallon-size freezer bag. Pour sauce over chicken. Seal and freeze. You can substitute thin pork chops for the chicken in this recipe. You may want to include a package of rice or egg noodles with this meal.*

# Hawaiian Chicken

6 boneless, skinless chicken breasts

½ cup ketchup

½ tsp. Worcestershire sauce

1 tsp. mustard

½ cup crushed pineapple with juice

½ cup brown sugar

**SHOPPING LIST FOR 10 MEALS**

30 lbs. boneless, skinless chicken breasts

5 cups ketchup

5 tsp. Worcestershire sauce

10 tsp. mustard

2 cans crushed pineapple

5 cups brown sugar

10 bags rice

A sweet way to enjoy your chicken.

◊ Put chicken in a 9 × 13 pan. Mix remaining ingredients together and pour over chicken. Bake at 350° for 45 minutes or stew in slow cooker for 4–6 hours. Serve over rice.

**FREEZING DIRECTIONS:**

*Place chicken in a freezer bag. Pour sauce mixture over chicken in bag. You may want to include rice with this meal.*

# Lemon Chicken

6 boneless, skinless chicken breasts

3 tsp. dried thyme

3 tsp. salt

1 clove garlic

1 cup lemon juice

**SHOPPING LIST FOR 10 MEALS**

abt. 30 lbs. boneless, skinless chicken breasts

abt. ⅔ cup dried thyme

abt. ⅔ cup salt

2 bulbs of garlic

10 cups lemon juice (80 oz.)

This chicken has quite the zing! Pair it with Dill-Lemon Rice for a flavorful meal.

◊ Mix spices and lemon juice in a bag. Add chicken breasts. If freezing, see directions below. Otherwise, marinate for several hours or overnight. Place in slow cooker for 4–6 hours on low. You can also bake or grill instead.

**FREEZING DIRECTIONS:**

*Place in a freezer bag. The chicken will marinate while thawing.*

# Red Chicken

5–6 boneless, skinless chicken breasts

1 cup ketchup

1 cup sugar

⅓ cup vinegar

⅓ cup soy sauce

1 Tbsp. mustard

1 tsp. garlic salt

**SHOPPING LIST
FOR 10 MEALS**

abt. 30 lbs. boneless, skinless chicken breasts

4 (24-oz.) bottles ketchup

10 cups sugar

3⅓ cups vinegar

3⅓ cup soy sauce

abt. ⅔ cup mustard

3⅓ Tbsp. garlic salt

10 small bags rice

A tangy, easy way to prepare chicken.

◊ Place chicken in slow cooker. Mix all other ingredients together and pour over chicken. Cook on low 5–6 hours. Serve over rice.

**FREEZING DIRECTIONS:**

*Place chicken in a gallon-size freezer bag. Mix all other ingredients together and pour over chicken. Seal and freeze. You may want to include a bag of rice with this meal.*

# Oregano Chicken

1 medium onion, cut into wedges

2 cloves garlic

6 boneless, skinless chicken breasts

2 cups water

2 Tbsp. balsamic vinegar

2 tsp. instant chicken bouillon powder

1 tsp. dried oregano

¼ tsp. crushed red pepper

2 tomatoes, sliced

6 cups cooked rice

It is possible to include meals with fresh produce. Keep the produce in the fridge and use this Make-Ahead Meal early in the month.

◊ In slow cooker, combine onion and garlic. Add the chicken breasts. In a bowl, stir together water, balsamic vinegar, bouillon, oregano, and crushed red pepper. Pour over chicken and cook on low for 5–6 hours or high for 3 hours. Place 1 cup of rice on a plate and place some tomato slices on top of rice. Place cooked chicken on top of rice and tomato and serve.

**FREEZING DIRECTIONS:**

*Mix all ingredients together and place in a gallon-size freezer bag. Include in separate sandwich bags 3 cups of long grain rice and 2 fresh tomatoes (don't freeze the tomatoes).*

**SHOPPING LIST FOR 10 MEALS**

60 boneless, skinless chicken breast (abt. 30 lbs.)

10 medium onions

20 cloves garlic

1¼ cups balsamic vinegar

abt. ½ cup instant chicken bouillon powder

2½ tsp. crushed red pepper

10 tsp. dried oregano

20 tomatoes

30 cups long grain rice

# Pineapple Coconut Chicken Curry

## 6–8 SERVINGS

½ large onion, cut in large chunks

½ large bell pepper, cut in large chunks

2 cloves garlic

1 (15-ounce) can coconut milk

2 Tbsp. ketchup

2 tsp. sriracha sauce

1½ tsp. salt

1 Tbsp. garam masala spice blend

1 Tbsp. curry powder

½ tsp. crushed red pepper flakes, optional for more heat

¼ tsp. black pepper

2 Tbsp. packed chopped fresh basil

4 large frozen chicken breasts

1 can pineapple chunks, drained

You might be surprised that this came out of your slow cooker. It's more than your usual soup or stew—and so much fun to eat.

Next time you're looking for a slow-cooker dish that's just not the same as all the others, this is the one for you. Make up a batch of rice to serve it with, and a delicious, company-worthy slow cooker dinner is served!

◊ In a large powerful blender or food processor, blend all of the ingredients except the chicken and pineapple chunks, until fairly smooth. (Doesn't have to be perfect, but it is a sauce, not a chunky stew!)

◊ Place the frozen chicken breasts and the pineapple chunks in the bottom of the slow cooker. Pour the curry sauce all over the top, cover, and turn on low for 6–8 hours. When the chicken is cooked through, shred it up with two forks and return it to the sauce.

◊ If the sauce is not as thick as you would like at this point (and it likely will not be!), make a little cornstarch slurry to thicken it: Mix 1½ Tbsp. cornstarch and 2 Tbsp. cold water together in a small glass until totally smooth. Stir this into the slow cooker and turn to high for another 15–30 minutes until it is as thick as you'd like.

*Serve the chicken and sauce over your favorite rice!*

You can blend the sauce ahead of time and store in the freezer until you need it. Thaw it in the fridge overnight, and then dump it in the slow cooker in the morning and continue with the recipe!

# Mexican Chicken

**6 SERVINGS**

1 (20-oz.) can enchilada sauce

2 Tbsp. brown sugar

¼ cup water

5 boneless, skinless chicken thighs

Tender shredded chicken that is smothered in a spicy and slightly sweet sauce.

◊ Mix together the enchilada sauce, brown sugar, and water. Pour into the slow cooker. Add the chicken and stir to coat. Cook on low 6–8 hours. Shred chicken with a fork while still in the slow cooker. Serve in tortillas with any of your favorite fixings, over rice, or however you like.

# Citrus Rubbed Chicken Tacos

**4 SERVINGS**

1 Tbsp. sea salt

1 Tbsp. ground black pepper

1 Tbsp. minced garlic

¼ cup minced sweet onion

2 limes, zested

2 lb. boneless chicken, any cut

2 Tbsp. extra-virgin olive oil

2 cups chicken broth

12 corn tortillas

This convenient pulled chicken recipe is perfect for gatherings at home or away. It is slow cooked, making it tender and juicy.

◊ Combine sea salt, black pepper, garlic, onion, and lime zest and rub on the chicken to coat evenly.

◊ Pour olive oil into a slow cooker and add chicken, flipping the pieces to coat both sides with oil. Pour in chicken broth and cover with lid. Cook on high heat for 4 hours or on low heat for 7–8 hours.

◊ Once the meat is tender and flakes easily, shred with a fork. Store warm and covered in the slow cooker until ready to use.

◊ Warm the corn tortillas on a skillet over medium heat. Fill with pulled chicken and serve.

# Chicken Parmesan

## 6 SERVINGS

2 lbs. chicken, boneless and skinless

1 (28-oz.) can crushed tomatoes

2 tsp. garlic, minced

1 (4-oz.) can sliced black olives

1 (4-oz.) sliced mushrooms

2 tsp. oregano

2 tsp. basil

1 tsp. thyme

1 cup shredded mozzarella cheese

This traditional favorite is tender and full of flavor. The only thing it's missing is the breading and frying!

◊ Cut the chicken into serving-size pieces and place in the slow cooker. Mix together tomatoes, garlic, olives, mushrooms, and spices. Pour over chicken and spread evenly. Cook on low 8–10 hours. Five minutes before serving, place a small mound of mozzarella on each piece of chicken. Cook until melted.

# Slow Cooker Teriyaki Chicken

**8 SERVINGS**

3 lb. boneless skinless chicken breast

¾ cup sugar

¾ cup gluten-free soy sauce

6 Tbsp. apple cider vinegar

1 tsp. ground ginger

1 tsp. minced garlic

¼ tsp. ground black pepper

1½ Tbsp. cornstarch

Slow cookers take the time to make great meals so that you don't have to. This sweet and tangy sauce seeps into the chicken as it cooks, creating a tender and juicy meal. Serve over cooked rice or in a sandwich or in a wrap. Picky eaters will love it.

◊ Wash the chicken and place in a 4-quart slow cooker.

◊ In a medium bowl, make teriyaki sauce by combining the remaining ingredients. Pour over chicken.

◊ Cover and cook on low for 4–5 hours or until chicken is tender. Shred chicken breasts with two forks and serve over cooked rice.

# Entrée: Pork

# Ham Barbecue

1 cup chopped celery

½ onion, chopped

¼ cup margarine or butter

wafer-sliced ham (enough to make 8 sandwiches; the sauce goes a long way, so you could add more if you like)

1 cup water

2 cups ketchup

2 Tbsp. vinegar

2 Tbsp. lemon juice

¼ cup Worcestershire sauce

¼ cup brown sugar

2 tsp. dry mustard

1 tsp. pepper

1 can tomato soup

A terrific recipe—great for large family gatherings.

◊ Sauté chopped celery and chopped onion together in margarine. Add the rest of the ingredients except ham and cook together for about 15 minutes or until heated through. If freezing, see sidebar. Otherwise, pour sauce over ham in a baking dish and bake at 300° for 30–40 minutes or in a slow cooker on low for 3–4 hours. Serve on buns or hard rolls.

**FREEZING DIRECTIONS:**

*Cool. Place ham in a freezer bag and pour sauce over. Include a bag of buns or hard rolls with this meal.*

## SHOPPING LIST FOR 10 MEALS

5 cubes margarine

abt. 20 celery stalks

5 onions

20 cups ketchup

1¼ cups vinegar

1¼ cups lemon juice

2½ cups Worcestershire Sauce

2½ cups brown sugar

abt. ½ cup dry mustard

abt. ¼ cup pepper

10 cans tomato soup

abt. 3 whole hams, sliced wafer thin

10 pkgs. buns or hard rolls

# Slow Cooker Korean Ribs

4 lbs. boneless, country-style pork ribs

1 cup brown sugar

1 cup soy sauce

½ cup water

3–5 whole jalapeño peppers (depending on how brave you are)

## SHOPPING LIST FOR 10 MEALS

40 lbs. boneless, country-style pork ribs

10 cups brown sugar

10 cups soy sauce

30–50 whole jalapeño peppers

Don't be surprised by the spicy ingredient. It just adds a little kick and great flavor!

◊ Place the ribs in a slow cooker. Mix together the brown sugar, soy sauce, and water. Pour over ribs. Add whole jalapeño peppers. (Don't cut them; leave them whole.) Cover and cook on low for 8 hours. These sound super spicy, and while they are cooking they will smell spicy, but it just adds a great flavor!

**FREEZING DIRECTIONS:**

*Place all ingredients except the jalapeños together in a gallon-size freezer bag. Include the fresh jalapeños with this meal to be added before cooking.*

# Creamy Pork Chops

## 6 SERVINGS

½ cup flour

2 tsp. salt

1½ tsp. ground mustard

½ tsp. garlic powder

6 pork chops, about ¾ inch thick

2 Tbsp. vegetable oil

1 (10.5-oz.) can cream of chicken soup

⅓ cup water

These tender chops are smothered in a savory and creamy sauce.

◊ Combine the flour, salt, mustard, and garlic powder. Dredge pork chops in mixture and brown on both sides in hot oil. Place chops in the slow cooker. Mix together soup and water. Pour over chops. Cook on low 6–8 hours. If desired, thicken pan juices and serve with the chops.

# Sweet and Savory Pork Chops

**6 SERVINGS**

6 pork chops, about
¾ inch thick

1 cup ketchup

½ cup water

1 medium onion,
chopped

½ cup brown sugar

1 (1-oz.) envelope
dry onion soup mix

The sauce will glaze the pork chops for a tender and decadent meal.

◊ Brown the pork chops on both sides. Place chops in the slow cooker. Mix the ketchup, water, onion, brown sugar, and dry onion soup mix. Pour over chops and mix to coat well. Cook on low 6–8 hours.

# Barbecue Pulled Pork Sandwiches

## 8 SERVINGS

4 lb. pork shoulder roast

3 Tbsp. paprika

1 Tbsp. salt

1 Tbsp. ground black pepper

1 tsp. garlic powder

1 tsp. dry mustard

⅓ cup liquid smoke

1 (20-oz.) bottle gluten-free barbecue sauce

A jar of barbecue sauce transforms any cut meat into a taste sensation in a snap. The secret is in the sauce, of course, so choose yours wisely when you whip up this simple meal.

◊ Coat a slow cooker with cooking spray. Place roast in slow cooker. Combine paprika, salt, pepper, garlic powder, mustard, and liquid smoke in a small bowl. Rub over the roast, covering all sides.

◊ Place lid on slow cooker and heat on high for 5–6 hours or low for 8–10 hours. Shred meat with two forks and strain meat. Top with barbecue sauce and serve on gluten-free sandwich bread or hamburger buns.

# Sweet Glazed Pork

## 8 SERVINGS

### PORK

1 tsp. Italian seasoning

½ tsp. salt

¼ tsp. ground black pepper

2 cloves garlic, crushed

4 lb. boneless pork (any cut)

½ cup water

### GLAZE

½ cup brown sugar

1 Tbsp. cornstarch

¼ cup balsamic vinegar

½ cup water

2 Tbsp. gluten-free soy sauce

This tender and juicy pork recipe is as easy to make as it is to eat. Let the slow cooker prepare the meal for you. Wait and enjoy this savory recipe as a sandwich or over rice.

◊ Combine Italian seasoning, salt, pepper, and garlic. Rub over roast. Place roast in slow cooker with ½ cup water. Cook on low for 6–8 hours.

◊ About 1 hour before roast is done, combine ingredients for glaze in small sauce pan. Heat and stir until mixture thickens. Pour over roast and cook for one more hour. Serve over rice.

Tip: NOT A RICE FAN?

Maybe you haven't found the one that you like. Before giving up, try Basmati, Jasmine, Arborio, short grain, brown, wild rice, and other varieties. You can even explore other grains like quinoa, amaranth, and polenta. If you are turned off by it because it's burdensome to make, let the rice cooker do the job for you. Spend around $20 and save yourself time and frustration.

# Spare Ribs the Easy Way

1 (6-oz.) can tomato paste

½ cup brown sugar

¼ cup vinegar

2 Tbsp. chili powder

1 Tbsp. hot sauce (I prefer Frank's)

3 tsp. granulated garlic

2 tsp. paprika

2 tsp. Worcestershire sauce

3 racks pork ribs

◊ Mix all ingredients except ribs in a slow cooker. Add ribs, making sure all sides of each rack of ribs is covered. Place in slow cooker. Cook on high for 4½ hours.

# Soups, Beans & Chili

# Chili

2 lbs. ground beef, browned and drained

2 quarts stewed tomatoes

1 pint salsa

30 oz. chili beans, drained

15 oz. kidney beans, drained

15 oz. pinto beans, drained

1 red bell pepper, chopped

1 green bell pepper, chopped

1 onion, chopped

4 Tbsp. brown sugar

salt to taste

cheddar cheese

This recipe will make enough for two families. Easy and satisfying—serve with cornbread and a green salad.

◊ Mix all ingredients together. Cook in large slow cooker 3–6 hours. To serve, top with shredded cheese.

**FREEZING DIRECTIONS:**

*Divide in half. Pour into gallon-size freezer bags. Include some shredded cheese with this meal.*

**SHOPPING LIST FOR 10 MEALS**

10 lbs. ground beef

10 quarts stewed tomatoes

5 pints salsa

5 large cans chili beans

5 (15-oz.) cans kidney beans

5 (15-oz.) cans pinto beans

5 red bell peppers

5 green bell peppers

5 onions

1¼ cups brown sugar

5 lbs. cheddar cheese

# Taco Soup

1 lb. ground beef, browned and drained

1 (15-oz.) can stewed tomatoes

1 (10-oz.) can tomato soup

1 (10-oz.) can vegetable soup

1 (15-oz.) can corn, drained

1 (15-oz.) can kidney beans, drained and rinsed

¾ cup salsa

1 cup water

2 Tbsp. taco seasoning

2 Tbsp. chili powder

A classic! Kids love eating tacos in a bowl.

◊ Mix all ingredients together. If freezing, see directions below. Otherwise, place in a large saucepan and cook until hot. Or heat in slow cooker on low for 3 hours. To serve, pour over crushed corn chips and top with sour cream and shredded cheese.

### FREEZING DIRECTIONS:

*Pour into a gallon-size freezer bag and freeze. Include a bag of corn chips, a carton of sour cream, and some shredded cheese with this meal. (Do not freeze sour cream.)*

### SHOPPING LIST FOR 10 MEALS

10 lbs. ground beef

10 (15-oz.) cans stewed tomatoes

10 (10-oz.) cans tomato soup

10 (10-oz.) cans vegetable soup

10 (15-oz.) cans corn

10 (15-oz.) cans kidney beans

abt. 2 quarts salsa

abt. 5 pkgs. taco seasoning

1¼ cups chili powder

10 small bags corn chips

10 small tubs sour cream

5 lbs. Cheese

# Easy Lemony Chicken Noodle Soup

**8–10 SERVINGS**

1 large onion, chopped

3 large carrots, chopped

3 large celery stalks, chopped

2 large garlic cloves, finely minced

3 cups cooked, chopped chicken meat

1 chunk parmesan cheese rind

2 bay leaves

½ tsp. dried oregano

8–12 cups good chicken stock

salt and pepper, to taste

½ pound egg noodles (or GF noodles, if needed), to serve

1–2 large lemons

I love a good soup. It is one of the easiest meals to throw together in your slow cooker for a quick, effortless meal any time of the year!

This recipe has two vital, game-changing ingredients. First is lemon juice. If you have never had lemon in your chicken soup before, you are missing out. It is so bright and fresh and amazing. Add a little, taste, and then add a little more until it is as lemony as you would like. (Or if not everyone is a lemon-lover, serve wedges on the side and squeeze into each bowl as you like!)

The next special ingredient is one you may never have used before, but I hope it becomes a second-nature thing. When you buy your big chunk of fresh parmesan cheese to grate (because you do, right? Please tell me you're not still buying that green can. Try the chunk. You will never go back!), save the rinds in a bag in the freezer. Whenever you make soup, or even a meaty pasta sauce, throw in a rind while it's cooking. It melts and saturates your dish with flavor in such an amazing way!

*One last note: A good chicken soup is only as good as the broth that it starts with. If you make homemade chicken stock, then you are step ahead of the game. Otherwise, buy the best stock you can find. It will make a difference!*

If you've never made homemade chicken stock, this is the perfect time to try it! Buy a rotisserie chicken, pull of all the meat, and save it for the soup later. Throw all the bones and stuff into a large pot and pour in just enough water to cover. Bring to a boil, reduce the heat to LOW, and simmer for 24–48 hours. Let the broth cool a bit, and then strain into jars and store in the fridge for up to a week (or freezer for up to 3 months!).

◊ Place everything except the noodles and lemon into a large crockpot and stir to combine. Cook on LOW for 8–12 hours, or HIGH for 4–6 hours. When you are almost ready to serve, cook ½ pound egg noodles according to package directions, and then drain and toss them with a bit of butter to keep them from sticking (and to flavor the soup even more!).

◊ When the soup is ready, squeeze the lemon into a small bowl, fish out the seeds, and then stir the juice into the soup, to taste. Taste for seasoning, adding salt and pepper and more oregano to taste, if you'd like. Find the parmesan rind and bay leaves and pull them out of the soup.

◊ To serve, place a generous scoop of noodles into each bowl and then ladle the bowl full of soup. Serve immediately and feel the comfort coursing through your veins with each bite!

*Store any leftover soup with the noodles kept separate to keep them from dissolving into mush in your soup!*

*This soup freezes beautifully for up to 3 months—without the noodles, of course. You could even freeze all of the ingredients except the noodles, lemon, and chicken stock in a large freezer bag and then just stir in the stock and continue the recipe when you are ready to make it!*

# Potato and Bacon Soup

3 cans chicken broth

2 cans cream of chicken soup

1 pkg. frozen cubed hash browns

1 lb. bacon, cooked and crumbled

1 small onion, chopped

½ tsp. pepper

¼ tsp. garlic powder

8 oz. cream cheese (not fat-free)

cheese for garnish

### SHOPPING LIST FOR 10 MEALS

30 cans chicken broth

20 cans cream of chicken soup

10 pkgs. cubed hash browns

10 lbs. bacon

10 small onions

5 tsp. pepper

2½ tsp. garlic powder

10 (8-oz.) bricks cream cheese

This is an easy version of this comfort food.

◊ Mix together chicken broth and cream of chicken soup. Add hash browns, bacon, onion, pepper, and garlic powder. Cook in slow cooker on low for 5–6 hours. About 1 hour before serving, add cream cheese and heat until thoroughly melted. Top with cheese.

### FREEZING DIRECTIONS:

*Pour into a gallon-size freezer bag. Seal and freeze. Include a package of cream cheese with this meal to be added at the end.*

# Slow Cooker French Onion Beef Soup

## 6–8 SERVINGS

4 Tbsp. butter

4 large sweet onions

3 large cloves garlic, minced

2 Tbsp. balsamic vinegar

1 Tbsp. worcestershire sauce

3 Tbsp. flour

7 cups beef stock

2 Tbsp. fresh thyme

salt & pepper, to taste

small (1½ pound or so) lean roast (or 1½ pounds of beef stew meat)

french bread, thick sliced

shredded gruyère cheese

Do you love french onion soup as much as I do? Do you look for it on restaurant menus and secretly cheer when you find it? Then I just might be your new best friend!

Not only is this french onion soup loaded with wonderful bites of tender beef, it is also incredibly easy and delicious! Serve this proudly to the meat lovers in your life. Enjoy!

◊ Turn your (6-quart or bigger) slow cooker on high, place the butter in the bottom, cover, and let it heat while you cut the onions in half and then thinly slice them and prep the rest of your ingredients!

◊ When the butter is melted, stir in the sliced onions, the garlic, balsamic vinegar, and worcestershire sauce. Cover again and cook on high for 1 hour, until the onions are soft and starting to brown on the edges.

◊ Dump in the flour, stirring well to coat, and cook for 5 minutes. (If you want, you can stop here, place the whole thing into the fridge overnight, and continue on in the morning!) Salt and pepper the stew meat generously and nestle into the slow cooker with the beef stock, thyme, and a touch more salt and pepper, depending on how salty your beef stock is. Cook on low heat for 8–12 hours, until the meat is tender, remove it from the pot, shred it up into bite-sized bits, and return to the soup.

◊ There are two ways to serve this soup! The traditional french onion soup way is to ladle the soup into oven-proof bowls and top with a thick slice of french bread and a generous sprinkle of shredded gruyère cheese. Place the bowls on a baking sheet and broil until the cheese is melted and golden, watching carefully.

◊ An easier way to serve this for a crowd is to leave the soup in the slow cooker and make a tray of cheese toasts to serve on top of each bowl. Preheat the oven to 450°F. Place thick slices of french bread or thick sliced baguettes in an even layer on a rimmed baking sheet. Top generously with shredded gruyère cheese. Bake for 5–10 minutes, watching carefully, until the cheese is melted and golden, and let everyone grab their own to top their bowls of soup or just to dip and eat as they go!

# Slow Cooker Smoky Ham & Bean Soup

## 8–10 SERVINGS

1 Tbsp. olive oil or bacon grease

1 large onion, chopped

3 large carrots, chopped

3–4 celery stalks, chopped

3 large cloves garlic, minced

2 cups diced ham

4 (15-ounce) cans beans, drained

4 cups chicken stock

1 (14.5-ounce) can diced tomatoes

2 tsp. ground cumin

1 tsp. chipotle chile powder, or smoked paprika

salt and pepper, to taste

Nothing but classic, simple comfort food here. This is incredibly quick and easy to throw together and fills every comfort-food-craving piece of your soul.

Busy, stressful winter days need this soup. Yes, I said need!

◊ Heat the oil or bacon grease in the slow cooker on HIGH while you chop up the veggies. Stir in the chopped onions, carrots, celery, and garlic to coat, and then stir in the rest of the ingredients.

◊ Cook on low 8–12 hours.

A little slow cooker tip for you—never open the slow cooker to check on the food. Every time you open the lid, 30 minutes should be added onto the cook time!

# Slow Cooker Cabbage Patch Soup

## 8–10 SERVINGS

2 lb. ground beef

½ tsp. garlic powder

1 large onion, chopped

1 cup chopped celery

¾1 head of cabbage, chopped

1 pound (about 3⅓ cups) frozen sweet corn

1 (64-ounce ) bottle V8 veggie tomato juice (I like spicy; use what you like!)

salt and pepper, to taste

It was always a good day, growing up, when we walked in the door to the smell of this amazing soup. It meant home, fall, and comfort. I could eat bowl after bowl of this hearty soup and not get tired of it . . . and I still can!

We grew up calling this soup "hamburger soup," but that name just doesn't do it justice. After much deliberation (and input from my family and friends!), we have decided to rename this delicious, hearty soup "cabbage patch soup." (Don't worry—my mom approves of the new name!)

Full of cabbage, beef, veggies, and a rich tomato broth, this soup has no rival. It is quick, easy, and a total crowd pleaser!

◊ In a large skillet, brown the ground beef over medium-high heat, seasoning it with salt, pepper, and the garlic powder, breaking it up into bite-sized chunks as it cooks. Once it is browned, remove it and drain off all but about 1 Tbsp. of the grease (if there was hardly any, add a bit of olive oil to the pan!). Sauté the chopped onion and celery in the pan, scraping up the bits of flavor on the bottom, until soft.

◊ Transfer the meat, onions, celery, and the rest of the ingredients (cabbage shrinks down substantially, so pack in the pot!) to a large slow cooker and cook on low for 8–12 hours.

*If you would rather make this on the stove, dump all the ingredients into a large pot, bring to a boil and reduce the heat to low, cover, and simmer for 2–3 hours, or as long as you'd like!*

*If you want to make this even easier to throw together, you can brown the meat, onions, and celery ahead of time and transfer them to a freezer-safe bag. Freeze for up to 3 months, and you are one step closer to an easy, delicious, no-fuss meal!*

*Optional: serve with noodles*

# Slow Cooker Calico Beans

**12–16 SERVINGS**

1 lb. ground beef, browned and drained

1 lb. bacon, cooked and crumbled

1 large onion, chopped

½ cup ketchup

⅓ cup firmly packed brown sugar

1 Tbsp. apple cider vinegar

1 Tbsp. worcestershire sauce

1 tsp. yellow mustard

1 tsp. salt

½ tsp. crushed red pepper flakes

1 (15-ounce) can tomato sauce

6 cups cooked mixed beans (if you like to use dried)

OR

2 (15-ounce) cans white beans, drained

1 (15-ounce) can kidney beans, drained

Calico beans are a satisfying cross between chili, baked beans, and a sloppy joe filling.

Full of a homemade barbecue-style sauce, lots of meat, bacon, and tender beans, these calico beans are meaty, tangy, salty, and deliciously perfect for any barbecue, picnic, or potluck you are heading to!

◊ Combine all ingredients in a large slow cooker, and stir gently until combined. Cook on low for at least 4 hours and up to 8 hours.

*If you like to use dried beans, you can make them ahead of time and freeze them in already portioned out amounts in freezer bags, making this almost as easy as opening a can for a fraction of the cost!*

# Creamy Cheese Soup

**8 SERVINGS**

5½ cups chicken broth

1 small onion, peeled and chopped

½ cup peeled and chopped carrots

½ cup chopped celery

¼ cup chopped red bell pepper

2 Tbsp. butter

1 tsp. salt

½ tsp. pepper

⅓ cup flour

½ cup water

1 (8-oz.) brick cream cheese, cubed and softened

2 cups shredded cheddar cheese

1½ cups water

So creamy and full of cheesy flavor.

◊ Mix together the first 8 ingredients in the slow cooker. Cover and cook on low 7–8 hours. Mix together the flour and ½ cup water until smooth. Stir into soup. Cook on high 30 more minutes or until soup is thickened. Stir in cream cheese, cheddar cheese, and 1½ cups water. Cook on low another 15 minutes or until heated through.

# Slow Cooker Coconut Curry Soup

**8 SERVINGS**

1 large sweet onion, chopped

2 Tbsp. green curry paste

4 cloves garlic, minced

1 Tbsp. minced fresh ginger

1 jalapeño, minced

¾ cup shelled English peas, chopped

1 cup sliced mushrooms

¾ cup carrots, sliced thin

8 cups vegetable broth

2 (14-oz.) cans coconut milk

2 Tbsp. gluten-free soy sauce

1 Tbsp. curry powder

3 Tbsp. sugar

1 Tbsp. turmeric

1 (14-oz.) can hearts of palm

1 (14-oz.) can bamboo shoots

¼ cup lime juice

salt and pepper

2 green onions, thinly sliced

¼ cup chopped fresh cilantro

This is a delicious curry soup. It is lower in calories, rich in nutrients, and extremely easy to make. Enjoy!

◊ Add all but the last 4 ingredients to a large slow cooker and gently stir. Cook on low for 6 hours, or on high for 3 hours.

◊ Before serving, stir in lime juice. Season with salt and pepper. Garnish with green onions and cilantro. Serve alone or over cooked rice or rice noodles.

# Slow & Low Leek and Potato Soup

**6 SERVINGS**

2 large leeks, washed, ends trimmed, thinly sliced

4 large potatoes, peeled and quartered

3 carrots, washed and chopped

2 celery stalks, chopped

2 cloves garlic, minced

salt and black pepper to taste

about 5 cups vegetable broth

sour cream

croutons

fresh parsley

This soup cooks for hours for a creamy and flavorful dish.

◊ Place leeks, potatoes, carrots, celery, and garlic in a slow cooker. Sprinkle with salt and pepper. Pour in vegetable broth, just enough to cover vegetables. Cover and cook on low for 6 hours.

◊ Purée soup in a food processor, working in batches, or with an immersion blender. Taste for salt and pepper. Ladle soup into bowls and garnish with sour cream, croutons, and parsley.

# Pasta
# &
# Sides

# Slow Cooker Beef Stroganoff

**4–6 SERVINGS**

**FOR THE HOMEMADE CONDENSED CREAM SOUP**

½ cup cold milk

⅓ cup flour (all-purpose or gluten-free substitute)

¾ cup beef stock

¼ cup milk

½ tsp. dried rosemary

½ tsp. garlic powder

½ tsp. onion powder

½ tsp. paprika

½ tsp. salt

½ tsp. pepper

**FOR THE REST**

1½ lbs. beef stew meat

2 Tbsp. worcestershire sauce

1 Tbsp. soy sauce

1 large onion, chopped

2 cloves garlic, minced

1 tsp. salt

½ tsp. pepper

1 lb. fresh mushrooms, halved or quartered

1 cup beef stock

1 cup sour cream

1 package egg noodles

I have been making this slow cooker stroganoff for years and years. It's one of those dishes that I just start craving when the weather turns and nothing will kick the craving until I make it.

Fortunately, it's delicious, and my family loves it too, so there's that!

◊ In a small bowl, whisk together the cold milk and flour until smooth. Set aside.

◊ In a small saucepan, whisk together the rest of the condensed soup ingredients and bring to a boil over medium-high heat. Once the mixture is boiling, slowly stream in the flour and milk slurry, whisking constantly, and continue to boil and whisk until the mixture is VERY thick (remember how thick a can of condensed soup is when you open it!).

◊ In a large slow cooker, stir together the stew meat, worcestershire sauce, and soy sauce until coated.

Spread into a layer on the bottom of the slow cooker. Dump the onions and garlic on top of the meat, season with salt and pepper, and then add the mushrooms. Dump in the homemade condensed soup and the beef stock, cover, and cook on low for 6–8 hours, until the meat is very tender.

◊ When you are about ready to serve, take off the lid, stir in the sour cream, and turn the heat up to high while you cook the noodles, stirring occasionally. Taste for seasoning and add more salt if needed. You can also stir in some fresh chopped parsley at this point, if you'd like!

◊ Cook the noodles according to package directions, drain, and toss with a bit of butter to keep them from sticking.

◊ Serve the stroganoff over noodles with lots of crusty bread to sop up the sauce!

*This condensed soup mixture makes about 1 can or 1½ cups' worth. You can make a much bigger batch and freeze in 1½ cup portions for easy use in any recipe that calls for condensed cream of anything soup! (Substitute chicken stock if you want!)*

*To make this gluten-free, use gluten-free tamari soy sauce and serve over rice or gluten-free noodles.*

# Meaty Spaghetti Sauce

## 6–8 SERVINGS

1½ lbs. ground beef

1 large onion, chopped

3 large cloves garlic, minced

½–1 lb. fresh mushrooms, quartered

1–2 (26-oz.) jars good marinara sauce (homemade or store-bought)

2 tsp. dried oregano

1 tsp. dried rosemary

½ tsp. crushed red pepper flakes

salt and pepper, to taste

1 parmesan rind*

You may not think spaghetti sauce is the most exciting thing you have ever seen a recipe for, but let me just tell you, this one is good. There is something about a big pot of tomatoey garlicky goodness that just screams "Yum!"

Throw this together in the slow cooker for the day, and dinner is practically served when you get home! (And I'll let you in on a little secret: sometimes I like to eat this delicious sauce by the bowlful and skip the noodles all together. But maybe that's just me?!)

◊ In a large skillet, brown the ground beef, remove from the pan (leaving as much grease as possible behind), and place into the bottom of a large (6-quart) slow cooker.

◊ Dump in the onion, garlic, mushrooms, and the marinara sauce (it's totally up to you if you want a thicker sauce with 1 jar, or a thinner sauce with 2!), and then stir in the spices.

*If you don't already save your parmesan rinds, start right now! When you have used up a chunk, place the rind in a freezer bag and freeze for—well, forever, practically. Just keep adding to the same bag every time you have a new rind. Add it to just about any savory, long-simmering dish, and you will be thrilled with the results!*

# Simple Sourdough Stuffing

**8–10 SERVINGS**

1 large loaf sourdough bread, cubed and left to dry overnight

1 ½ cups butter

1 ½ Tbsp. poultry seasoning

1 large onion, chopped

2 cups chopped celery

2 tsp. salt

1 tsp. pepper

2–3 cups chicken stock

Everyone has their favorite Thanksgiving side dish, and this is one of mine.

Second only to my fresh cranberry apple sauce, this buttery sourdough stuffing is the perfect accompaniment to the moist turkey and rich mashed potatoes and gravy.

Does anyone else love Thanksgiving food as much as I do?!

◊ Preheat the oven to 350°F. Butter a 9×13 baking dish. Set aside.

◊ Heat the butter and poultry seasoning in a large skillet over medium-high heat. Add in the onions and celery and sauté for 5–10 minutes, until soft. Add in about 1/2–2/3 of the stale bread cubes (as much as your pan can hold) and sauté them in the butter until starting to turn golden and absorb the butter.

◊ Stir in the rest of the bread and dump the mixture into the buttered dish. Pour 2–3 cups of chicken stock all over the bread (more if you like wetter dressing, less if you like drier dressing!) and place in the oven to bake for 30–45 minutes until golden.

*You can stuff some of this into your turkey if you'd like! And another way to make this ahead is to place everything in a slow cooker instead of into the buttered pan and heat on low for as long as you need until you serve it!*

# Pineapple Cinnamon Squash

**6 SERVINGS**

3 lbs. Hubbard squash or banana squash, peeled and cubed

1 (8-oz.) can crushed pineapple

½ tsp. ground cinnamon

⅓ cup brown sugar

1 Tbsp. butter, cut into small pieces

Autumn is in the air when this dish is served. Such a sweet and tasty side dish.

◊ Place the squash in the slow cooker. Mix the other ingredients together and pour on top. Stir to coat. Cook on low 6–8 hours, or until squash is tender.

# Slow-Cooked Apple Butter

**MAKES 6 HALF PINTS**

10–12 cooking apples, chopped (14 cups)

2 cups apple juice

3 cups sugar

1½ cups cinnamon

½ tsp. ground cloves

*Apple butter will keep several weeks in refrigerator.*

This is a nice hands-off recipe. It's easy to prepare and turns out great every time.

◊ Core and chop unpeeled apples. Combine with apple juice in slow cooker. Add sugar. Cover; cook on high setting for 4 hours or low setting for 10 hours.

◊ Remove apples from slow cooker and put apples into blender; blend on high speed until smooth. Return apples to slow cooker. Add cinnamon and cloves. Cook on low setting for 1 hour or until mixture reaches desired consistency. For very thick apple butter, remove lid while cooking.

◊ Ladle into 6 sterilized half-pint jars, leaving 1/2 inch headspace. Adjust lids. Process in boiling water bath 10 minutes.

# Lemony Steamed Artichokes

**4 SERVINGS**

2 cups boiling water

2 tsp. salt

8 peppercorns

2 stalks celery, cut up

¼ cup lemon juice

4 artichokes, stalks and tough leaves removed

I love how tender and flavorful these turn out. The lemon juice gives them just the right tanginess.

◊ Combine the water, salt, peppercorns, celery, and lemon juice in the slow cooker. Place artichokes stalk side down in the slow cooker. Cook on high 4–5 hours.

# Baked Stuffed Potatoes

**6 SERVINGS**

3 medium potatoes

1 (10-oz.) can cream of chicken soup, mixed with ½ can of water

1 (15-oz.) can chili (whatever is your favorite)

10 oz. or 2 cups grated cheese

sour cream to top

A meal in itself. So good!

◊ Cut potatoes in half, leaving skins on. Place in bottom of slow cooker. Pour cream of chicken mixture over potatoes, and cook for 1 hour. Pour can of chili over potatoes and cook for 6 hours.

◊ Top with grated cheese and cook for 20 minutes more. Serve with sour cream.

# Cheesy Potatoes with a Twist

## 8 SERVINGS

6 slices bacon, chopped

4 large potatoes, peeled and thinly sliced

½ cup grated Gruyère cheese

1 tsp. salt

½ tsp. pepper

1½ cups heavy cream

This is not your typical scalloped potatoes. The unique cheese makes it extra special.

◊ Cook the bacon and drain. Place alternating layers of ¼ of the potatoes, ¼ of the bacon, and ¼ of the cheese. Sprinkle each layer of potatoes with salt and pepper. Pour the cream over all the layers. Cook on low about 8 hours.

# Whole Wheat Rolls

### 4–6 SERVINGS

1 pkg. or 2 Tbsp. yeast.

1½ cup warm milk

2 cups bread flour

1 cup potato flakes

1 tsp. salt

1 Tbsp. oil

Homemade goodness in every bite.

◊ Mix all ingredients well to form sticky dough.

◊ Put a buttered paper cup in middle of slow cooker to prevent dough from moving to the center and becoming doughy.

◊ Add sticky dough in piles around cup.

◊ Cook on high for 2 hours.

# Perfect White Rolls

**6–7 SERVINGS**

6–7 frozen bread
rolls, thawed

Never fail, always tasty.

◊ Butter slow cooker and place a buttered paper cup
in middle of slow cooker to prevent dough from
moving to the center and remaining doughy.

◊ Place rolls around cup, allowing room to rise. Cook
on high for 2½ hours or until bottom and sides of
rolls are brown.

# Desserts

# Berry Bread Pudding

**8 SERVINGS**

6 cups cubed dense white bread

1 cup fresh raspberries

2 cups heavy cream

2 cups milk

1¼ cups sugar

6 eggs

1 Tbsp. vanilla

Rich and decadent, this dish could be used for breakfast, brunch, or dessert!

◊ Layer half of the cubed bread in a well-greased slow cooker, and sprinkle with half of the berries over top. Repeat the layers, ending with berries. Whisk together the cream, milk, sugar, eggs, and vanilla. Pour into the slow cooker over the bread cubes and berries, and gently push down the bread to evenly moisten. Cook on high about 2–3 hours or until a knife inserted in the center comes out clean. Remove the lid and cook another 15 minutes. Serve with whipped cream, milk, or ice cream.

# Lemon Sponge

**6–8 SERVINGS**

1 cup sugar

¼ cup flour

¼ tsp. salt

¼ cup lemon juice

1 Tbsp. lemon zest

3 eggs, separated

1 Tbsp. butter, melted

1 cup milk

1 Tbsp. powdered sugar

Tart and sweet and melt–in–your-mouth good.

◊ Mix together sugar, flour, and salt. Stir in lemon juice, lemon zest, egg yolks, butter, and milk. In a separate bowl, beat egg whites until stiff peaks form; fold into lemon mixture. Pour into a greased bowl and cover tightly with aluminum foil (secure with an elastic band). Place bowl in the slow cooker and pour in enough water to come 1 inch up sides of bowl. Cover and cook on high 4–5 hours or until topping is set and light and fluffy. Sift powdered sugar over sponge before serving.

# Brownies and Berries

**8 SERVINGS**

1½ sticks butter, melted

1½ cups sugar

⅓ cup cocoa powder

3 eggs

1 tsp. vanilla

⅛ tsp. salt

½ cup milk chocolate chips

1 Tbsp. butter to grease the bottom of the pot

If you love crunchy and gooey, these are the brownies for you. They are great for à la mode ice cream and berries.

◊ Turn the slow cooker on high, and add one Tbsp. butter to melt and coat the slow cooker pot with.

◊ Mix all ingredients. Pour into buttered slow cooker, and cook for 3 hours. The edges should be crunchy and the middle gooey. Serve with your favorite berry.

# Gooey Brownies

**8 SERVINGS**

1 box brownie mix (and ingredients listed on the back)

ice cream of choice

chocolate syrup

Here is a chance to use your favorite mix and make it easier.

◊ Prepare your favorite brownie mix according to the directions on the back of the box. Pour batter into a preheated, buttered slow cooker. Cook for 3 hours on high. Serve with ice cream and top with chocolate syrup.

# Cherry Pot Cobbler

**8 SERVINGS**

2 (21-oz.) cans cherry pie mix

1 box yellow cake mix

1 stick of butter

Whipped cream

maraschino cherries

A favorite in the crock pot or in a Dutch oven.

◊ Mix together pie mix and cake mix in a slow cooker. Do not overmix.

◊ Top with one stick of butter, cut into slices. Cook on high for 3 hours.

◊ Top with whipped cream and maraschino cherries. Serve.

# Peanut Butter Piles

**20 SERVINGS**

6 oz. peanuts, shelled

4 chocolate bars

10 miniature chocolate peanut butter cups

The combination of chocolate and peanut butter is addicting. An easy favorite.

◊ Layer the ingredients in a slow cooker in the order listed. Melt for 20 minutes on high. Mix together and spoon onto buttered tray. Refrigerate 2 hours before serving.

# Hot Spiced Cider

**10–12 SERVINGS**

4 cups (one 32-oz. container) Tazo chai concentrate

8 cups good apple juice

4 large cinnamon sticks, broken in half

2 tsp. whole cloves

1 tsp. whole peppercorn

10 whole cardamom pods, lightly crushed

pinch of salt

I know hot spiced cider might not seem like the most exciting thing to find in a cookbook, but let me tell you . . . this stuff is amazing!

So warm and cozy and a nice kick of spice and caffeine (you can use decaf chai if you want!), you may never go back to the plain old stuff after trying this chai cider! (gluten-free)

◊ In a large slow cooker, stir together all of the ingredients, and then heat on low for several hours until nice and hot!

*This spiced cider can be reheated several times. Make a full batch on a cold day, and if it doesn't get finished off, just store it in the fridge and reheat it the next day!*

# GLUTEN-FREE
# Hot Cranberry Pineapple Punch

## 12–15 SERVINGS

3 cups cranberry juice

3 cups pineapple juice

1½ cups water

¼ cup brown sugar

1½ tsp. whole cloves

2 large cinnamon sticks

pinch of salt

1 cup fresh (or frozen) unsweetened cranberries

My aunt Judi has a wonderful recipe for "percolator punch" that I have always been thrilled with. For so many years, I avoided making it because I have never owned a percolator.

One day, I smacked myself in the face when I realized my slow cooker would work just as well. Goodness, I had been missing out!

This is my favorite hot fall and winter party punch. Everyone loves it and it makes the house smell amazing. It's a win-win!

◊ In a medium pot, stir together all of the ingredients and heat over medium-low heat until it is hot. Reduce heat to very low and simmer for as long as you'd like (it will taste even better as it sits), or at least until the cranberries start to burst and the punch is nice and hot!

This hot punch can easily be mixed up in a pitcher in the fridge for up to a week before heating, or can be heated in the slow cooker all day for a hands-off treat. Serve hot!

# About The Authors

# Lyuba Brooke

LYUBA BROOKE grew up surrounded by talented chefs. For her tenth birthday, she received her first cookbook as a gift and has been cooking and baking ever since. Although her first recipe, on her tenth birthday, turned out to be a disaster, she did not give up and learned to cook with passion. In 2011, she put her passion for cooking and creating recipes to use by sharing her creations at willcookforsmiles.com.

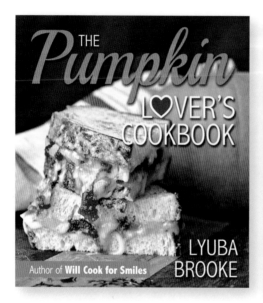

WWW.WILLCOOKFORSMILES.COM

# Carlene Duda

CARLENE DUDA is a published author, culinary writer, teacher, cook, and baker. Her award-winning recipies have been published and appear in newspapers and copyrighted by C & H Sugar Company. Carlene attended Ricks College (BYU-Idaho) and Brigham Young University. Carlene lives in Puyallup, Washington, with her family.

# Kristena Eden

KRISTENA EDEN has always loved to cook with her kids, especially as a fun, creative activity to share, learn, and participate in to bring her family together. Her parental goal in cooking was to teach communication and life skills together in one activity. Through this bonding, she has developed great relationships with her children, who are all excellent cooks.

WWW.THEWRITEBOOK.COM

# Suzie Roberts

SUZIE ROBERTS is one of those busy mothers who knows how challenging (not to mention boring!) putting dinner on the table night after night can be. She started her own Make-Ahead Meal Group in 2004 and became such a believer in this method of cooking that she decided to share her succes with others. She continues to come up with creative and fun ways to give her more time to spend with family and friends. Suzie lives in Perry, Utah, with her husband, David, and their five children, Kyra, Kuen, Tatem, Bryson, and Mylee.

ONTHEGOCOOKBOOK.BLOGSPOT.COM

# Christi Silbaugh

CHRISTI SILBAUGH is the self-educated chef and author of three cooking blogs including *Mom, Whats for Dinner*, *Gourmet Cooking for Two*, and *Zero Calorie Life*. She writes for foodie media giants Glam Media and Federated Media and works for Fast Forward Events, covering food and wine events in San Diego. Since 2009, she has created and posted over 1,000 gluten-free recipes. She lives with her family in California.

WHATSFORDINNER-MOMWHATSFORDINNER.BLOGSPOT.COM

# Brenda Stanley

BRENDA STANLEY is a former television news anchor and investigative reporter for the NBC affiliate in eastern Idaho. She has been recognized for her writing by the Scripps Howard Foundation, the Hearst Journalism Awards, the Idaho Press Club, and the Society of Professional Journalists. She is the author of four other books—three novels and one cookbook. Brenda is an adjunct professor at Idaho State University in the Mass Communication department. She is a graduate of Dixie College in St. George, Utah, and the University of Utah in Salt Lake City. She is the mother of five grown children, including two sets of twins (born twenty months apart—yes, four kids under the age of two), and she is now a grandma. Brenda and her husband, Dave, a veterinatian, live on a small ranch near the Snake River with their horses, sheep, chickens, and dogs.

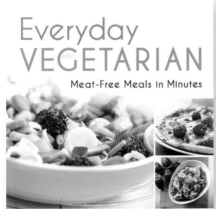

WWW.TALESOFTHEDINNERBELLE.COM

# Annalise Ree Thomas

With four kids, a large extended family, and a passion for feeding others, Annalise is no stranger to finding ways to simplify life in the kitchen. There is nothing that makes her happier than hearing from someone who was once intimidated in the kitchen "I made this! It was great, and now I'm feeling more confident in trying more homemade recipes!"

Annalise spends her time in the kitchen and exploring the beautiful Olympic Peninsula of Washington, where she lives with her family. If you want to find her, look in her kitchen or at one of the many beautiful beaches nearby watching her children play and combing for beach glass!

WWW.SWEETANNAS.COM

# Michele Vilseck

MICHELE VILSECK is a mother, entrepreneur, and health enthusiast. She enjoys creating in all of its forms including writing, cooking, artwork, and teaching. She has been gluten-free for ten years. She lives in Michigan with her family.

# Index

## B

## C

## D

## E

## F

## G

## H

## I

## L

# Notes

# Notes

Let your slow cooker do the hours of work for you with these savory home-cooked meals. Whether you're making entrées like Carne Asada Tacos or desserts like Lemon Sponge Cake, all you need is a little planning and prep work to prepare wholesome dishes that are full of flavor. Spend a few minutes preparing, and then let your slow cooker do the rest!

eBook
$0.99
shelfie.com
with purchase

FRONT TABLE
BOOKS

CEDAR FORT
Publishing & Media

AN IMPRINT OF CEDAR FORT, INC.

ISBN 978-1-4621-1988-2     USA $19.9

9 781462 119882

5

WWW.CEDARFORT.COM